Iconic
American Muscle Cars
1968-1971

By

Don Narus

www.newalbanybooks.com

IMC11818

Contents

Chapter	Page

Printed and published in the United States of America by LuLu Press, Inc. Raleigh, NC
Distributed by New Albany Books, Palm Harbor, FL

Iconic
American Muscle Cars
1968-1971
By
Don Narus

Published and printed in the United States of America, type set in Arial on premium white, by LuLu Press, Inc, Raleigh, NC.
No part of this book may be reproduced in any format without the consent of the author, except for reviews where credit is given to the author and / or the work. Copies of this book can be purchased directly from the publisher, LuLu.com.

Copyright 2018
ISBN 978-1-387-42430-6

Published by
LuLu Press, Inc. Raleigh, NC 27607

Distributed by
New Albany Books, Palm Harbor, FL 34684

First Edition

Narus, Donald (Don)
   1. Performance cars, 2.Muscle Cars, 3.AMC, 4.Buick, 5.Chevrolet, 6.Dodge, 7.Ford ,
   8.Pontiac, 9. Plymouth, 10. Oldsmobile

Acknowledgments
and Photo Credits

The images reproduced in this book are digital, direct download digital jpg images of various sizes. Some are originally black and white (usually Factory or Archived Photos). Others are color converted to black and white using a greyscale process. While all images were necessary to the content of this book their quality varies. The best images available at the time for the examples shown, were chosen. Every attempt was made to provide the best image. We also realize that photos are subjective. If better images or a conversion process becomes available after initial publication, they will be used in later revised editions.

Every attempt was made to give credit to each original photo. If we missed someone, I apologize, it was not intentional. Please know that every photo is important to the content of this book. Thanks to the following for making this book possible. The Detroit Public Library Auto Archives, Yahoo images, Google images, Wkikipedia.com, Hyman Ltd, Auto-Lit.com, Flicker.com, flickerriver.com, conceptcarz.com, Mecum.com, Barrett-Jackson.com Daniel Schmitt & Co, Motortopia.com, e.walpapers.eu, yourtube.com, GTAall.com, carbuzz.com car24news.com,CustomClassics,com,IMCDb.org, Fine Art America, Pintrest.com, RK Motors, Ocities.org, Cars-On-Line.com, Carscoops.com, Powernation, Barn Finds, Mecum.com, Top Speed, Shevells Muscle, Car garage, Arrive in style, Barrett-Jackson, Conceptcarz.com, Supercarz.com, Mind Over Motor, wikimedia commons, You Tube Ford Horizon 3, Gielda Kiasykow, pl, GTAs-Mods.com, MustangandFords.com, Muscle Car Drive, emwheelage.org, Happy Days Dream Cars, AutoTrader Classics, Automobile Magazine, Velocity.com, HotRod.com, Classis Car Fusion, How-Stuff-Works.com, Classicoldcars.net, HotRodNetwork My Classic Garage, Wallalphacoders.com, WheelsAge.org, Lingenfelter Collection, American Modern, Motor Authority, Wallpaperup, No Car No Fun, Muscle Cras World, Flemings Ultimate Garage, Classics By Ferrell, ClassCars.com, MotorShout, AllPar.com, CarDominion, TopClassicCarsForSale.com, Cars with muscle, Hot Rod Network, Classic Cars For Sale On Line. Gearheads.org, Alphacoders.com, www.gieldaklasykow.pl

Front Cover: Photo from CarDomain.com

Rear Cover: Photo from alphacoders.com

Introduction

The rumble; the roar; burning tires screeching across the pavement. This was the era of raw, unbridled, unleashed power. Street legal, 429 cubes at 500 hp, 0-60 4.5 seconds. Zoom-Zoom. It only lasted a few years, until the oil embargo. In the blink of an eye it was over. No more fast and furious. This book deals with the best of the best, the Muscle Cars that reached their zenith in 1968 through 1971. We have chosen the Buick GSX Stage 1, the Camaro COPO 427, the Charger 426, the Javelin AMX 401, the Mustang "9" Boss 429, the Olds Hurst 442, the 1971 Trans Am 455HO, the 1969 GTO 400HO Judge and the Plymouth Hemi Cuda 426.. The Iconic American Muscle Cars.

The Buick GSX aka GS appeared mid year 1970 and only 678 were produced, The Stage 1 was a 455cu in V-8 producing 360hp. It was said that the GSX could out perform the Pontiac GTO. The Olds 442 W-30 and the Plymouth Hemi Cuda. The GSX was available in two colors only: Saturn Yellow and Apollo White. In 1969 Chevrolet, with demand from its key dealers, began installing 427 cu in V-8s Code L-72 in select Camaro's, identified as COPO (Central Office Production Orders). There were two versions of the big block V-8s, 9560 and 9561. The 9560 used an all aluminum Big Block, ZL-1 and the 9561 used a cast iron, solid-lifter Big Block L-72. The engines were rated at 430hp, but with a tinkering (exhaust changes and tuning) horsepower was increased to 500.

The second generation Oldsmobile Cutlass was introduced in 1968. The horsepower race was heating up and Oldsmobile decided to partner with Hurst Performance and create the Hurst/Olds 442. It was equipped with 455 cu in V-8, 390Hp; 0-60 in 5.4 seconds. Only 515 were produced. All cars were painted a special silver color with black racing stripes and white pinstripes. In 1969 Pontiac upped the anti with its second generation GTO. With the introduction of the "Judge", a 400HO V-8 with Ram Air III rated at 366hp, and a optional 370hp Ram Air IV. Of the 72,287 GTO's sold that year, 6,833 had the Judge package The second generation Firebird Trans Am was introduced in mid-year 1970, offering a Ram Air III at 335hp and a optional Ram Air IV rated at 345hp. Only 3,196 were sold that model year.

The undisputed king of the road was Mustang. In 1969 Ford introduced the Mustang Boss"9", (Boss 429), A special modified 4-speed Cobra Jet Mustang, reworked by Kar Kraft of Dearborn, Mi to accept the large 429 cu in. Rated at 375hp, its actual output was 500hp, and was capable of reaching 175 mph. In 1970 Plymouth introduced the "Hemi Cuda", available as a coupe and convertible. Equipped with a 426 cu in Hemi V-8, rated at 425hp. .In 1971 Dodge introduced the Third Generation Charger, and part of the series was the R/T 500 equipped with a Hemi 440 cu in V-8, rated at 350hp. Only 63 Hemi R/Ts were built that year.
Not to be outdone AMC unveiled their second generation sports car in 1971. It was longer, wider, lower and heavier then the previous generation. The Javelin AMX fitted with: a 401 cu in V-8, rated at 335hp, could do the quarter mile in 14 seconds.

The nine Muscle Cars featured in this book were the baddest street machines of their day, but it all came to an abrupt end with the oil embargo of the 1970's. All of a sudden auto makers were scrambling for 4 cylinder econo boxes. The horsepower race was over.

Don Narus

Buick GSX Stage1
1970

Buick unveiled the Gran Sport in 1965, an option in the Skylark series.. It featured a 400 cu in V-8 (actually a 401 cu in, but based on General Motors restrictions as to size , Buick called it a 400 cu in) The big block V-8 produced 325hp. More than 15,00 Skylarks with the GS option were sold. In 1967 the Gran Sport became a Skylark sub series. After the initial year sales fell as Muscle Car competition increased. Buick's Gran Sport was considered a Luxury Performance Car compared to the other popular muscle cars. Buick got serious in 1969 when the horsepower race heated up. In 1969 introduced the Stage 1 option, which delivered 340hp. Production was limited to 1,500 cars.

The engine used in the initial Stage 1 option proved to problematic. Improving the engine and overcoming the initial problems. Buick introduced a new improved Stage 1 option consisting of a 455 cu in, 360hp V-8 (360hp was the advertised rating, while dynamometer testing shown the engine capable of 471hp). The new option was standard in a new model, the GSX a 1970 mid model year introduction. Only 678 GSX'x were produced in 1970. This was Buick's answer to the Pontiac GTO, the Olds Hurst 442 and the Plymouth Hemi Cuda.

The 1970 GSX Stage 1 is comparable to the and some would say, surpasses the Plymouth 426 Hemi Cuda. The 1970 GSX was available in two colors only. Saturn Yellow and Apollo White. It had a full body black racing stripe, a rear spoiler and red pin stripes and a hood mounted tachometer.. Standard equipment included: black bucket seats, floor shifter, wide oval tires, close ratio steering, anti-sway bars front and rear, and a quad linked suspension with a limited-slip differential. A 3-speed manual transmission was standard with optional 4-speed manual and full automatic.

In 1971 and 1972 the GSX became an optional performance package available on any GS model. The GSX lasted until 1972 . In its last year only 44 were sold.

Introducing automobiles to light your fire.

The Gran Sports. From Buick 1970.
They're the cars you've been asking us to make.
This one's the GS455 equipped with the Stage I performance package.
If it's performance you want, the GS455 Stage I has it.
A 455 cubic-inch engine. With a high-lift cam and four barrel carburetor which breathes through real air-scoops to add performance.
A cooling system that should never overheat.
And four on the floor is available. Or an improved 3-speed automatic transmission.
Maybe it's the name Buick, with all the goodness and confidence that goes with that name, that really gets you.
Whatever it is, the GS455 Stage I has it. And so do all the Light Your Fire Cars from Buick 1970. See them.

Now, wouldn't you really rather have a

1970 Buick.

Buick GSX Stage 1

The 1970 Buick GSX Stage 1 powered by a 455 cu in, 370hp V-8, was priced at $5,489 and only 400 were sold. The Stage 1 Was said to be equal to or better than the Hemi Cuda. The shaker hood, rear spoiler, Rallye wheels, and special striping was standard.

A close-up look at the dual air scoop shaker hood. Hood pins, spoiler and GSX badging.

The 1970 GSX held its own on the track or on the street. Matched up well with the Hemi Cuda

10

The 1970 Buick GSX Stage 1 interior featured: vinyl covered bucket seats, floor shifter center console sport steering wheel, racing mirrors (left side remote controlled) HydraMatic 400 optional. Seat belts, head rests and wall-to-wall carpeting were standard.

The GSX Stage 1 engine. A 455 cu in, bored to 0.40 over to 464 cu in, without the factory fan,air cleaner and muffler, and fine tuning the carburetor bench tested at 381.7hp.

1970 Buick GSX

Wheelbase: 112 inches	Engine: 455 cu in, 370hp, Stage 1, V-8		3-speed manual trans*
Model		Price	Built
44637	Hardtop Coupe	$4,881**	400
44667	Convertible Coupe	5,067**	N/A

**Base price plus $1,196 Stage 1 package.
*4-speed manual and 400 Turbo Hydramatic optional
Note: Dynamometer test on the Stage1 indicated 481.7 gross hp.

Standard Equipment

Hurst floor shifter, functional hood scoops, chrome red filled lower body molding and wheel well moldings, five spoke chrome wheels, blackedout grille, rear spoiler, special striping and badges, Vinyl bucket seats, seat belts, wall-to-wall carpeting, center console all black interior and exterior color choices of Saturn Yellow and Apollo White.

Optional Equipment

Am Radio, AM/FM radio with stereo player, Tilt steering wheel, power steering, power brakes, remote control outside mirrors, soft ray tinted glass, four-way or six way power seats, Electric door locks, clock, and electric trunk release.

Production, pricing and equipment information from Standard Catalog of Buick by Mary Sieber and Ken Buttolph and www.wikipedia.com

Z is for "Zap!"

Translation: a 302 V8 with mechanical lifters, hi-performance cam, aluminum intake manifold, Holley 4-barrel.

Plus: multi-leaf rear springs, heavy-duty shocks, new white-lettered tires on 15 x 7 wheels.

And a Hurst shifter for the 4-speed.

While you're at it, why not add the new 'Vette type 4-wheel disc brakes?

By now you know the mean streak isn't just painted on—it's built in.

CHEVROLET

Putting you first, keeps us first.

We've got a mean streak.

Z/28 Camaro.

Camaro COPO 427
1969

The first generation Camaro arrived in dealers showrooms in September 1966. The Camaro was Chevrolet's answer to Fords Mustang. It was available as a 2-door coupe, 2+2 hardtop and a convertible with a choice of six cylinder or V-8, coupled to a 3-speed manual transmission. By 1969 there were 12 different engines available together with a choice of 4-speed manual, 2-speed Powerglide automatic, and 3-speed Turbo Hydramatic automatic transmission. By 1968 there was a choice of trim packages; the RS, SS and Z-28. The RS and SS were appearance packages while the Z-28 was a performance package, with a 302 cu in, 350 hp V-8

Initially the Z-28 was a race track only offering, however, the Special Products Division came up with a plan to make it street available. In order to do this they had to convince Chevy's General Manager, Pete Estes to allow production of a one-off Z-28 convertible that was built for Estes to drive. Once driven Estes ordered the Z-28 into production.

In 1969 General Motors mandated that Chevrolet make available a V-8 no larger than 400 cu in., however Chevrolet dealers such as Don Yenko were offering dealer installed 427 cu in V-8s. Which prompted Chevrolet to offer the 427 in Camaro's, using a ordering process called COPO (Central Office Production Orders) usually reserved for fleet special orders. Two ordering numbers were created 9560 and 9561. Number 9560 offered a all aluminum 427 cu in V-8 called the ZL-1 designed for drag racing designed by drag racer Dick Harrell which could be ordered through Fred Gibb Chevrolet, of La Harpe, Illinois. Those produced with the ZL-1 were to be used for NHRA stock car racing. Each ZL-1 was hand assembled and took 16 hours to produce. The engine cost $4,000. A total of 69 ZL-1 Camaro's were built in 1969.

The COPO number 9561 offered the 427 cu in L-72 solid lifter, cast iron big block V-8. It was underrated at 425 hp, but with a little tinkering could be boosted to 500hp. This is the engine chosen by Don Yenko Chevrolet. In 1969 estimates of 900-1000 L-72 Camrao's were built, most of these became the Yenko Camaro's and were badged as such.

The Camaro became a formidable challenger to the Mustang and captured top honors in the SCCA Trans Am Champion races. Mark Donahue and Roger Penske were the top Camaro drivers. All this ended with the oil embargo of the 70's. By 1973 manufacturers were scrambling to come up with a compact Econo box. The emphasis was on MPG not HP. The Horsepower race was over.

1969 Camaro COPO 427 Coupe

1969 Camaro COPO 427 Coupe, no frills no nonsense, all power. Priced at $3,174.65* The rear spoiler was a $32. option. An estimated 900-1,000 were built.

* estimated price, based on base V-8 price plus cost of 427 engine.

Camaro COPO interior featured vinyl upholstery, bucket seats, seat belts, head rests, floor shifter, wall to wall carpeting. A center console, power seats and windows were optional.

1969 Camaro COPO 427 Convertible

Camaro COPO 427 Convertible fitted with the L-72 V-8 carried special badging. The striping, rocker molding and wheel opening trim, alloy wheels, rear quarter trim, hidden head lights and hood louvers were part of the optional SS/RS trim package .

1969 Camaro COPO 427 Yenko Coupe

Camaro COPO 427 Coupe fitted with the L-72 V-8 were sold through Don Yenko Chevrolet had special striping and badaging designating it as a Yenko S/C Coupe. Included in addition to the striping, a rear spoiler, alloy wheels, raised letter tires, raised hood and front air dam.

The Camaro 427 COPO V-8 was rated at 425hp, but with tinkering could be pushed higher.

1969 Camaro COPO 427

Wheelbase: 108 inches	Engine: 427 cu in, 425 hp, V-8*	3-speed manual trans.**	
Model		Price	Built
67	Convertible Coupe	$3,388.65^	N/A
37	2-door Coupe	3,174.65^	1,000^^

*The performance 427 was available as 425hp L-72 and 376hp ZL-1.
** Available options; 4-speed manual, 2-speed Powerglide, 3-speed Turbo Hydra-Matic.
^ Estimated price: base V-8 plus cost of L-72 engine.
^^ Estimated

Standard Equipment

Functional air scoop hood,dual exhaust, special front and rear suspension, heavy-duty radiator and temperature controlled fan, quick ratio steering, Rally wheels,white letter tires, 3.73 ratio axle, Rally stripes, all vinyl strato bucket seats with head rests, shoulder seat belts, wall-to-wall carpeting, astro ventilation system, heater and defroster, remote outside mirror, side marker lights, interior courtesy lights

Optional Equipment

Special front bumper, Electric clock, Heavy-duty clutch, Center console with courtesy light, Power door locks, Power brakes and steering, Power windows, Six way power seats, Special instrumentation, Light monitoring system, AM push button radio, AM/FM radio, Am/Fm stereo radio, Rear manual antenna, Cruise control (automatic drive required), Quick response steering, Tilt steering column, Sport steering wheel, Power convertible top.

Production, pricing and equipment information from the Standard Catalog of Chevrolet by Pat Chappell and Wickipedia.com.

NOW A DODGE CHARGER WHITE HAT SPECIAL.

If you take a car that's breaking sales records all over the country...

Add the options people want most...
And cut the price...

Will more people buy it?

Let's find out.

Dodge White Hat Special Charger.

Now you can get a super deal on America's Super Car. The special low White Hat package price includes:
• Vinyl roof in black, white, tan or green • Simulated, wood-grained steering wheel • Hood-mounted turn signals
• Light group • Outside, remote-control rearview mirror
• Whitewall tires • Deep-dish wheel covers.
Look for the special "White Hat" sticker.
It's your ticket to a money-saving deal.

How can you resist it?

Get **DODGE** *fever*

Dodge CHRYSLER MOTORS CORPORATION

24

Dodge Charger / Coronet R/T Hemi 426
1969

We highlight the Charger R/T Coupe and the Coronet R/T Convertible for 1969, the best year for both cars.

The Dodge Charger first appeared in 1966 as a mid-sized sporty show car filling a slot between the "Pony Car" and the "Personal Luxury car". It was a fastback based on the Coronet platform, using a lot of the in stock Coronet parts and powered by a 426 cu in 425hp Hemi V-8.. The Charger R/T first appeared in 1968, offering a 426 cu in optional Hemi. 475 were sold with a price tag of $4,110.75*,. Buyers were split that year between the 4-speed manual and the Torqueflite automatic (211 to 264 respectively). In 1969 powered by a 426 cu in, 425hp Hemi V-8. The Charger R/T was priced at $4,196.75* and 20,057 were sold. In 1970 it sold for $4,315.75* and only 63 Charger Hemi R/T's were sold. (Sales declined due to high insurance costs). and in 1971 there was a moderate price increase of $66, but sales continued to drop. There were no more R/T's after 1971.

The Dodge Coronet R/T Hemi convertible first appeared in 1967 as a separate series offering both a coupe and convertible. The standard power plant was a 440 cu in, 350hp, V-8 coupled to a Torqueflite automatic transmission, A 425 cu in , 425hp Hemi V-8 was optional. Only 3 R/T convertibles were sold with the 426 package. The price tag was a hefty $3,899, which was $457 more than the standard R/T. In 1968.the price tag for a Hemi equipped Cornet R/T rose to $4,325 and only 8 were sold. In 1969 the Coronet Hemi R/T convertible got a price bump of $166. Of the total combined sales of 7,338 R/T Coronets only 10 were Hemi R/T convertibles. !969 would turn out to be the best year for the Hemi Coronet R/T rag top. 1970 would be the last year for the Hemi Coronet Convertible. Total Coronet R/T convertible sales that year were 296 and only 2 were Hemi equipped. A modest price increase of $178 made no difference buyers preferred the Hemi Charger coupe which was only $62 cheaper. But if you wanted a convertible the Hemi Coronet was your only option.

The Chrysler 426 cu in, Hemi V-8 was a powerhouse. With less cubic inches than the 440 it created 450 ft lbs of torque and 425hp. The " Rallye Dash" provided a 150mph speedometer and Tic-Toc-Tach with clock. It was the engine of choice at NASCAR. In 1970 a Hemi Charger had ten wins, more than any other competitor. It gave Dodge Charger driver Bobby Isaac the National Championship. The Dodger Hemi Charger was a force to recon with. Today the rarest of the Hemi R/Ts are the Cornet Convertibles with less than 30 built over a four year run and can fetch six figures at auction.

1969 Dodge Charger R/T Hemi 426 Coupe

The 1969 Dodge Charger R/T Hemi 426 available only as a Coupe; this was year two of the second generation Charger. Styling changes included a new grille, restyled roof panel and tail lights. According to Mopar Authority Galen V. Govier only 232 were built. Priced at $4,230.

1969 Dodge Charger R/T interior shown with vinyl bucket seats with adjustable head rests, ,standard floor shifter (3 or 4 speed manual), sport steering wheel, padded dash with wood grain inlay, seat belts and wall-to-wall carpeting. Full set of functional gauges. Radio, optional.

1969 Dodge Coronet Hemi 426 Convertible

The Charger R/T was a Coupe only, if you wanted a Hemi convertible you ordered a 1969 Dodge Coronet R/T Hemi 426 Convertible. All the standard features of the Charger with a soft top. Hood, grille and sheet metal were slightly different. Priced at $4,378, only 10 built.

1969 Dodge Cornet R/T Hemi 425 convertible interior shown here featured: vinyl covered bucket seats with adjustable head rests, seat belts, center console with Hurst floor shifter, with 4-speed manual trans, power windows, sport steering wheel and wall-to-wall carpeting.

The 426 Hemi R/T Engine. 450 ft lb Torque, 425hp. Street legal, rubber burning beast of a car.

Dodge R/T 426 Hemi

Wheelbase: 117 inches	Engine: 426 cu in, 425hp, Hemi V-8		3-speed manual trans.*	
Model		Price		Built
X529	Charger R/T Coupe	$4,230**		232^^
WS27	Coronet R/T Convertible	$4,378**		10^^

*Available options: 4-speed manual trans, and Torqueflite Automatic.
**Price determined by adding cost of 426 Hemi to base model price.
^^Number built with 426 Hemi provided by Mopar Authority Galen V. Govier

Standard Equipment

Vinyl covered bucket seats with adjustable head rests, floor shifter, padded dash, seat belts, hood scoops, Rallye instruments, sport steering wheel, Tic Toc Tach, sure grip differential, heavy duty radiator, hood pins, dual breaker distributor, full carpeting, special striping, simulated side panel air scoops, dual exhausts with chrome tips, R/T handling package, heavy duty manually adjusted brakes,

Optional Equipment

The 426 cu in Hemi was optional only in the R/T cars. It cost $718 in the Coronet and $648 in the Charger.. Torqueflite automatic and 4-speed manual were optional, Other options included: Air Conditioning, Power steering, Power brakes, Power front discs, Power seats, Power windows, Electric clock, Sure-grip differential, AM Radio, AM/FM Radio, AM/FM multiplex stereo, AM/8track stereo, Cruise control, Sun roof, (Charger), Rallye suspension, Wood grain steering wheel, Tilt steering column, Chrome 14 inch rims and White wall tires.

Note

NASCAR speedway no holds bared war was taking place in order for dodge to compete against the more aerodynamic Fords, Dodge introduced the Daytona Charger. A elongated fiberglass nose was mounted over the standard front grille and a huge roof high spoiler was mounted on the rear deck. The clumsy looking contraptions cold achieve speeds up to 200mph, An advantage that gave Bobby Isaac the top prize in 1969. In order to comply with NASCAR rules Dodge produced 1,000 Daytona Chargers to be sold to the general public.

Pricing, production, and equipment information from the Standard Catalog of Chrysler by James T. Lenzke and www.wikipedia.com.

American Motors and Mark Donohue specially prepared and modified the new Javelin-AMX, so you don't have to.

Last season, in Trans-Am Road Racing, Mark Donohue was racing for us and winning.

Obviously, we were thrilled. We had never won in Trans-Am before. And that gave us an idea.

Why not ask Donohue to take some of his special preparations and modifications for the track, and incorporate them into a Javelin for the road.

And that's what he did.

The new Javelin-AMX is a completely redesigned performance car. From its fast, glacial slopes on the outside. To its cockpit console on the inside.

But first and foremost, as a true performance car, it is built around the principle that air pressure has to work for you. Not against you.

It has a body that is wider and lower on the outside. With a wider rear tread for better stability.

It has a front wire-mesh grille screen that is flush with the wind.

A rear spoiler specially designed by Donohue.

New intake manifolds for deeper breathing. New exhaust manifolds to reduce back pressure. A new optional cowl-air induction system. And an optional front spoiler.

Of course, the new Javelin-AMX also has everything else you'd normally expect on a performance car.

A standard 360 CID V-8 engine that develops 245 horsepower. Or an optional 4 barrel carb for 285 horsepower.

A standard 3-speed all synchromesh floor shift transmission with an 11" heavy duty clutch. Or an optional 4-speed with a Hurst shifter.

An optional heavy duty suspension system, big tach, and gauges. Standard fat Polyglas™ tires, mag style wheels, and a couple of things you wouldn't expect.

New optional ventilated-rotor front disc brakes to fight brake fade. And a new optional 401 CID engine that generates 330 horsepower.

Mark Donohue will be driving the new Javelin-AMX in next season's Trans-Am.

You could be driving it right now.

If you had to compete with GM, Ford and Chrysler, what would you do?
◥◣ American Motors

32

AMC Javelin AMX 401
1971

Sometime in 1965-1966 AMC was looking for a way to rid itself of it's stodgy, econo image. AMC designers came up with two proposals. One was a 2-place Fiberglass GT Fastback the AMX, the other was a 4-place Fastback the AMX II. Both were built as concepts and made the show circuit. The idea was to appeal to the growing youth market. The AMX was a big hit and based on public reaction both cars were approved for production. The 2-place model continued as the AMX, the 4-place model was now called the Javelin. The AMX originally fiberglass was now made of steel. The AMX was powered by a 290 cu in, 225hp V-8, slated to compete with the Ford Thunderbird and the Chevrolet Corvette. The Javelin was powered by a 232 cu in Six or a 343 cu in V-8. The Javelin was designed to compete with the Ford Mustang. It came in two trim levels, the basic and the SST. Both models debuted in 1968. The Javelin sold 55,124 units in 1968. In 1969 it sold 40,675 of which 28, 286 were V-8's. In 1970 the Javelin 'Trans Am' and the Mark Donohue SST were introduced. Total production was 30,034 of which only 4,100 were six cylinder models.

In 1971 the Javelin was completely restyled. The front fenders were raised with a bump out, the roof was a twin canopy configuration with a rear air spoiler that formed the upper lip of the rear window and full width tail lights. The interior was also completely redesigned into a airplane styled cockpit with an aircraft type instrument panel. The AMX became the top of the line Javelin , standard power was a 304 cu in, 180hp V-8 with optional 360 cu in, 198hp V-8 and 401 cu in, 255hp V-8. A "Go Package" was an available option which included the 401 V-8 with four barrel carb, dual exhausts, Hood decal, Rally-Pac instrumentation , a handling package, Cowl-air carburetor induction, heavy duty cooling, twin grip differential, Polyglas raised letter tires, steel stylized wheels and space saver spare. The package cost $411.

The 1971 Javelin was the second generation; it was wider, lower longer and heavier than previous years. The wheelbase was increased to 110 inches. The new Javelin featured an injection molded grille. It also had many racing modifications such as a fiberglass hood with induction cowl and a flush stainless grille. Testing by the Penske Racing Team clocked the AMX with a 401 cu in V-8 in the quarter mile at 14 seconds reaching 93 mph, using low-lead , low octane gas. Only 2,054 Javelin AMX's were sold in 1971, the exact number of 401's is unknown.

The Javelin AMX continued in production through 1974 with little change. In 1972 only two models were available the SST and the AMX.. A total of 26,184 Javelins were sold in 1972, 2,729 were AMXs. In 1973 government mandated emission controls were incorporated,still a AMX Javelin with a 401 could do 0-60 in 7.7 seconds. Sales improved to 5,707 AMX units (there is no breakout for those equipped with 401's). In it's final year 1974, the Javelin AMX sold 4.980 units (no breakout for 401 equipped cars). Muscle cars were on the way out, even the mighty Mustang was scaled down to a Mustang II with four cylinders.

It's nice to know you're driving the winner.

Last year a specially modified Javelin AMX beat every other car in its class in the Trans Am racing series. In the last race of the year at Riverside, we blew everybody off the track finishing one, two, three.

This year the AMX has blown up another storm by clinching its second Trans Am Championship in a row.

But when we call the AMX a winner, we're talking about more than racing, we're talking about the way the AMX looks inside and out.

We're talking about the room you have even in the back seats; the stability of the car at all speeds; the nice balance of performance and comfort.

And only American Motors makes this promise: The Buyer Protection Plan backs every '73 car we build and we'll see that our dealers back that promise.

AMERICAN MOTORS BUYER PROTECTION PLAN

AMC Javelin
We back them better because we build them better.

1971 AMC Javelin AMX 401

The all-new redesigned 1971 Javelin AMX 401 shown with special striping, deep dish rims, wide tires, rear deck spoiler, and AMX badging. It was priced at $4,186.95 with "Go Package".

Javelin AMX single head lamps, driving lights, stainless mesh grille and front air dam. The new design featured a twin canopy roof panel with a air spoiler that framed the back window..

Racing versions of the AMX Javelin had a smaller steering wheel, a single contoured bucket seat, close ratio floor shifter and built in roll cage. Large rear deck spoiler, extended gas filler pipe, side exhaust pipes, hinged back glass, and heavy duty springs and shocks.

Javelin AMX interior featured full set of gauges, including tachometer, dished sport steering wheel with safety hub, cloth covered bucket seats with center console, floor shifter, engine turned dash insert panel, padded dashboard and wall-to-wall carpeting.

The 1971 Javelin 401 cu in ,335hp, V-8 with 4 barrel carb coupled to a Borg-Warner T-10 4-speed manual trans with Hurst floor shifter could do the quarter mile in 14 seconds.

1971 AMC Javelin AMX 401

Wheelbase: 110 inches   Engine: 401 cu in, 335hp, V-8   3-speed manual transmission*

Model		Price	Built
7179-8	Javelin AMX Coupe	$3,688**	2054^

* 4-speed manual, 3-speed automatic and 3-speed "Torque Command" optional
** Price calculated using base model price plus cost of 401 V-8
^ Total AMX model produced, no break out for 401 equipped cars.

Standard Equipment

Rear facing air induction hood, wire mesh grille, custom steering wheel, color keyed full carpeting, locking glove box, high back bucket seats, floor shifter, center console, electric clock, rear deck spoiler, slot wheels , glass belted tires, and command air ventilation.

Available Options

Power brakes, power steering, power door locks, power windows, power front disc brakes, locking gas cap, electric clock, front and rear bumper guards, cruise control, engine block heater, heavy system, tinted glass, tinted windshield, headlight delay system, body side molding, AM push button radio, AM/FM push-button radio, AM/FM multiplex stereo radio, AM/radio 8-track, leather bucket seats, corduroy fabric bucket seats, center console, tilt steering column, custom wheel covers, turbo cast wheel covers , wire wheel covers, styled steel wheels, electric wiper washers.

Pricing and production information from Standard Catalog of American Cars by John A. Gunnell and wikipedia.com.

Mustang "9" Boss 429
1969-1970

In 1969 Chevrolet released the COPO Camaro, which featured a 427 cu in, V-8 high performance racing engine. The 427 was specifically designed for racing, but responding to dealer pressure, it was made available by special order in the Camaro (Central Office Production Order 9560 and 9561- COPO). The 427 cu in, V08 was rated at 430hp but could be tweaked to 500hp. The 427 cu in V-8 pushed the price of the Camaro 2-door hardtop to $3,175.

Ford upped the ante when it introduced the Mustang Boss 429 (aka Mustang "9") in February of 1969. It was the big brother to the Boss 302. Originally It was designed as a racing engine for Trans Am racing. In order to comply with NASCAR and Trans Am racing rules the 429 had to be available to the general public. The new second generation Mustang bodies had a larger engine bay and was suitable for the 429, and so the Boss 429 was born. The Boss 429 cars were assembled at the Kar Karft assembly plant in Brighton, Michigan.

The 429 cu in , V-8 was rated at 375hp with 450 ft lbs of torque, but equipped with dual Holley 850 CFM four barrel carbs was capable of 650hp. The engine used four-bolt mains, forged steel connecting rods, aluminum heads with a modified Hemi style combustion chamber, which Ford called "cresent" . The heads were mounted dry (no head gaskets). Each cylinder, oil passage, and water passages had "O" rings seals. The Boss 429 was a brute, it could do 0-60 in 7.1 seconds, and a quarter mile in 14.1 seconds at 102mph. It had a maximum speed of 130mph, which is not note worthy by today's standards.

On a banked track or as a Trans Am racer is was superb. However as a street rod or drag racer not so much. The car was nose heavy and light in the rear end, with 450 ft lbs of torque it burned a lot of rubber. But once it reached 3,000 rpm, it was a bullet. Unrestricted it was capable of reaching over 175mph.

The Boss 429 was a unique Mustang unlike its siblings, For one it had a manual choke situated next to the ignition switch, next to the choke was the hood scoop fresh air control knob. The 85 amp battery was mounted in the trunk, chromed mag 500 wheels were standard along with 15 inch raised letter polyglas tires. In addition there was a high capacity engine oil cooler, 65 amp alternator, power steering with oil cooler, 4-speed gear box, power front disc brakes, rear drum brakes, traction-lock rear axle, 3.91 ration special high performance suspension, front spoiler, center console, high back bucket seats, dual racing mirrors, visibility group, and deluxe seat belts and special badging. The Boss 429 V-8 was priced at $4,294.76 $1,215 more than the Camaro..

Ford continued the Boss 429 for 1970, with five new exterior colors. The interior was available in black or white and black, The hood scoops were all painted matte black. The Hurst shifter was also standard. The Boss 429 was offered for two years only: 859 were sold in 1969 and 499 were sold in 1970.

1969 Mustang "9" Boss 429

The 1969 Mustang "9" Boss 429, was the king of the muscle cars. Powered by a 429 cu in, rated at 375hp (actual output 500hp) with 450 lb of torque. Unrestricted it was capable of 175mph. Dual exhausts. 4-speed manual with floor shifter, Shaker hood, rear quarter air intakes and Rallye wheels were standard. It was priced at $4,294.76. Total built 857.

The 1969 Mustang Boss 429 with its larger hood scoop, front air dam, deep dish Raylle wheels and wide raised letter tires presented a very aggressive stance.

A close-up look at the grille, driving lights, front air dam. Note: slightly raised rear deck lid

The basic body and modified front clip were shipped from the Ford Rouge plant in Dearborn, Michigan to Kar Kraft in Brighton, Michigan for final assembly.

The 1969 Mustang Boss 429 cu in, rated at 375hp (actual output 500hp)..Some dyno tests have shown as much as 600hp capable of 175mph. With 450lb of torque, heavy-duty cooling, two four barrel carbs, four-bolt mains, forged steel crank, forged steel connecting rods and modified Hemi combustion chambers (Ford called them "crescent" chambers). Its a brute.

The 1969 Mustang Boss 429 interior 2+2 fastback featured molded door and quarter trim panels. Heavily padded, vinyl covered, rear seats that accommodated two passengers.

Padded dashboard with wood inserts, full set of gauges, sport steering wheel, floor shifter, center console with seat buckle holder, full carpeting, vinyl covered bucket seats, standard.

1970 Mustang Boss 429 Fastback

The 1970 Mustang Boss 429 received minor facelift. New grille with air induction vents, rear quarter panels without air vents, it was priced at $4,393.76. This was last year for the 429.

The new grille featured single head lights, air induction vents, and cantilever shaker hood. The rear quarter panels air vents were gone. Rallye wheels and raised letter tires; standard.

1970 Mustang Boss 429 interior featured: high back vinyl covered bucket seats, center console with floor shifter, sport steering wheel, padded dash, full set of gauges, seat belts, padded door panels, rear molded quarter panels and wall-to-wall carpeting.

1969 Mustang Boss 429

	Wheelbase: 18 inches	Engine: 429 cu in, 375hp V-8		4-speed manual trans.
Model			Price	Built
63A	2+2 Fastback Coupe		$4,294.76*	859

*Pricing source Hemmings Book of Mustangs.

1970 Mustang Boss 429

	Wheelbase: 108 inches	Engine: 429 cu in, 375hp V-8		4-speed manual trans.
Model			Price	Built
63A	2+2 Fastback Coupe		$4,393.76*	499

*Price reflects a $99 increase in the base V-8 2+2 Coupe. as shown in the Standard Catalog of Ford by John A. Gunnell.

Standard Equipment

Exterior: High capacity engine oil cooler, 65 amp alternator, 85 amo trunk mounted battery, power steering with oil cooler, 4-speed transmission, power front disc barkes, traction-lock rear axle. High performance suspension, front spoiler, Raised letters 15" Polyglas tires, Magunum 500 chrome plated wheels, Dual side view mirrors. and Rear-end sway bar.

Interior: Vinyl covered high back bucket seats, seat belts, wood grain décor trim,center console, floor shifter, visibility group, 130mph speedometer, tachometer, sport wood grain steering wheel.

Available Options

A ir conditioning, AM radio, AM/FM stereo radio, stereo-sonic tape system, tilt steering column, tinted glass, remote control left side view mirror

Pricing, production and equipment information from Standard Catalog of Ford by John A. Gunnell and the Encyclopedia of American Cars by the Editors of Consumer Guide.

Oldsmobile Hurst 442
1968-1969

In 1968 Oldsmobile joined with Hurst Performance Research Corporation to produce the Hurst/Olds. A step up from just adding a optional Hurst shifter to a model. Stock 442's installed with special drive trains and ram-air were delivered to Demmer Engineering of Lansing, Michigan where the Hurst components were added. The process included a special paint scheme, Peruvian Silver with black accent and white pin stripes with red wheel wells. real walnut dashboard trim, Dual-Gate Hurst shifter, H/O logos and a mini console. The standard engine was a 455 cu in, 390hp, V-8. Painted fire engine red, matching the wheel wells. Front disc brakes, heavy duty cooling and sport suspension.

The 1968 Hurst/Olds 442 performed very well doing 0-60 in 5.4 seconds and the quarter mile in 13.9 seconds at 103mph. A total of 515 were produced that year (459 Holiday Coupes and 56 Sport Coupes). All were equipped with Turbo 400 automatic transmissions.

Very little was changed for 1969, mostly to the grille where a division bar was added to split the grille. The deck lid had inlets for the taillights, wing windows were eliminated from Holiday Coupes and Convertibles. The hood featured dual hood scoops which had "H/O 455" emblems applied, special striping and a pedestal rear spoiler was added along with chrome plated wheel rims and dual racing mirrors. A steering lock ignition switch was added along with front seat headrests. All cars were painted Cameo white with Frost gold striping. The 455 cu in V-8 was slightly detuned, now rated at 380hp it was the same engine that was installed in 1968 A/C equipped cars. The engine received a special intake manifold, chrome vale covers and a vacuum operated air cleaner damper that allowed fresh air from the hood scoop into the carburetor. A total of 914 Hurst/Olds were produced in 1969 including 6 prototype sport coupes and 2 promo convertibles.

The two 1969 Hurst/Olds 442 convertibles were built for Hurst Performance to be used as promo cars. They were shuffled around the country to racing events promoting Hurst products and featured Lynda Vaughn, "Miss Golden Shifter" who was perched on a platform attached to the rear deck of the car holding on to a giant shifter mock-up.

Oldsmobile temporarily dropped the Hurst/Olds model after 1969, due to GM's dropping of the 400 cu in V-8 limit for the 1970 model year. Dropping that limit permitted all divisions to install larger engines in their muscle cars. For 1970 the 445 cu in 365 hp V-8 or optional 370hp V-8 became standard in all 442's. Oldsmobile planned to bring back the Hurst/Olds as a lower priced model in the 442 series. It was later introduced mid-year as the Rallye 350. The next Hurst/Olds would not be introduced until 1972.

1968 Oldsmobile Hurst 442 Holiday Coupe

The 1968 Hurst/Olds 442 Holiday Coupe was powered by a 455 cu in, 360hp, H/O V-8. It could do 0-60 in 7 seconds and a quarter mile in 15.13 seconds at 9emph. The engine was rated at 115mph. It was priced at $3,340 and 459 Holiday Coupes were sold.

1968 Hurst/Olds 442 interior featured: padded dash, deep dish sport steering wheel, Hurst floor shifter, pleated vinyl front bucket seats and rear bench seat, and wall-to-wall carpeting.

1968 Hurst/Olds 442 Sport Coupe

1968 Hurst/Olds 422 Sport Coupe, had all the features of the Holdiday coupe but was priced at $3,277, only 56 were built. It had a special front fender racing stripe with Hurst 442 logo.

Hurst/Olds 455 cu in, 390hp, V-8. Cars so equipped could do 0-60 in 7 seconds and the quarter mile in 15.13 seconds. Note: the dual air induction hoses.

1969 Hurst/Olds 442 Holiday Coupe

Oldsmobile added brighter colors and bold racing stripes to the 1969 Olds / Hurst 442 Holiday Coupe. It was priced at $4,500 and a total of only 913 of the 455 Holiday Coupes were built.

The 1969 Hurst/Olds (HO) 455 featured special badging, racing mirrors and quad headlights.

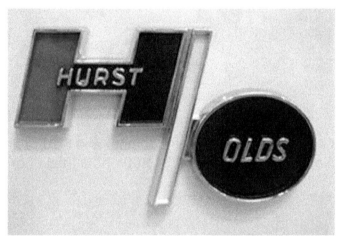

The 1969 Hurst/Olds 455 interior featured: vinyl covered bucket seats, sport wheel, center console with Hurst shifter, wood dash panel insert, full gauges, wall-to-wall carpeting.

The 1969 455 cu in, 380hp, W-46 with 500lbs of torque. With a unique intake manifold. chrome valve covers, and a vacuum operated air cleaner lid, which allowed air from the hood scoop directly into the carburetor. H/O emblems appeared on the sides of the Hood scoops.

1969 Oldsmobile Hurst 442 Sport Coupe Prototype

1969 Olds Hurst 442 Sport Coupe prototype. Only six were built for engineering evaluation.

1969 Oldsmobile Hurst 442 Convertible Promo Car

1969 Olds Hurst 442 Convertible , the Hurst promo car, only two were built for use by Hurst Performance Products to promote its products; specifically the Hurst Shifter.

1969 Olds Hurst promo convertible with "Miss Golden Shifter"" Lynda Vaughan. Hurst used the car to promote its products at racing events around the country.

1968 Oldsmobile Hurst 442

Wheelbase: 112 inches   Engine: 455 cu in, 390hp, V-8   3-speed manual transmission**

Model		Price*	Built
4487	Holiday Coupe	$3,340	459
4477	Sport Coupe	3,277	56

* price calculated using base model price plus cost of 455 V-8
** 4-speed manual and a turbo automatic were options

1969 Oldsmobile Hurst 442

Wheelbase: 112 inches   Engine: 455 cu in 380hp, V-8   3-speed manual transmission**

Model		Price*	Built
4487H	Hurst/Olds Holiday Coupe	$4,500	906
4477H	Hurst/Olds Sport Coupe	prototype	6
4467H	Hurst/Olds Convertible	promo car	2

*price from Standard Catalog of American Cars by John A. Gunnell
** 4-speed manual and a turbo automatic were options.

Standard Equipment

(1968)Real walnut dash insert,Special paint scheme, H/O badging, Vinyl bucket seats, Hurst dual-gate shifter, mini-console, Disc brakes, Heavy-duty cooling, sport suspension, Tic-toc-tac, wood grained steering wheel, Power front disc brakes. (1969) Special Paint scheme, H/O badging, Hurst shifter, Steering lock ignition switch, Standard headrests front seats, Twin hood stripes, Dual hood functional air scoops, rear pedestal spoiler, Chromed wheel rims, Racing mirrors.

Optional Equipment

(1968) Power brakes, Power steering, Air conditioning, Electric clock, Cruise control, Tissue dispenser, Guidematic headlight control, Floor mats, Remote control side mirror, Door edge guards, AM radio, AM/FM stereo radio, Am/FM radio, Stereo tape player, Power antenna, Power trunk release. (1969) Power steering, Air conditioning, Tinted glass, floor mats, Sports console, Rear defogger (coupes), Tilt steering wheel, Rallye instruments, Stereo tape player, AM/FM radio, AM/FM stereo radio, Power antenna, Power seats, Cornering lights.

Pricing, production and Standard and Optional equipment information from Standard Catalog of American Cars by John A. Gunnell and www.wikipedia.com

1971 PONTIAC
FIREBIRDS
TRANS AM / FORMULA / ESPRIT / FIREBIRD

Pontiac GTO Judge and Trans Am
1970-1971

Pontiac had two contenders in the Muscle Car category. The GTO and the Trans AM, both competed with three other manufacturers and themselves. Originally the GTO was an option package for the Pontiac Tempest. It became its own model and series in 1966 based on the Tempest sheet metal. It was powered by a 389 cu in V-8. Standard equipment included a 4-barrel carburetor, dual exhausts, heavy duty shocks, springs and stabilizer bar. Three models were available: a 2-door coupe, a hardtop coupe, and a convertible coupe. It was 'the' muscle car up to 1970 when its strongest competitor was the Pontiac Trans AM. It has been said that the GTO was the car that started the Muscle Car trend.

For 1970 GTO continued to use Tempest sheet metal, but it used a Endure rubber nose that featured dual oval cavities that housed mesh grille inserts and a GTO emblem on the left insert. Standard equipment included; vinyl bucket seats, padded dash, hood with twin air scoops, heavy duty clutch, beefed up springs and shocks, dual exhausts, wall-to-wall carpeting, courtesy lights, deLuxe steering wheel, a 3-speed manual floor shift transmission and black fiberglass tires. In 1970 General Motors lifted the ban on limiting mid-size cars from using engines larger than 400 cu in, The GTO Judge package first introduced in 1969 was again available with a standard 400 cu in Ram Air V-8 with "T" handle Hurst floor shifter. An available option was the 455 HO V-8. Rated at 360hp with 500 ft lbs of torque, and coupled to a 4-speed manual trans and 3.31 axle could do a quarter mile in 14.8 seconds and 0-60 in 6.6 seconds. The GTO "Judge"was primarily a hardtop coupe and a few convertibles. The number of cars equipped with the HO 455 is unknown..

Firebirds were first introduced in 1967 to compete with the Mustang and Camaro. Two models were available, a coupe and a convertible. The Firebird Trans AM was introduced in 1969 as a separate model and series. With to versions available the hardtop coupe and the convertible. In 1970 the Trans Am was available only as a hardtop coupe. The standard engine was a 400 cu in 335hp Ram Air V-8 with a 4-speed manual transmission. The Ram Air V-8 was capable of doing the quarter mile in 13.9 seconds and 0-60 in 6.4 seconds. With the 400 cu in size limit lifted by GM in1970, the 455 cu in. V-8 was a late available option. 3,108 with the 400 cu in Ram Air III were sold and 88 of the Ram Air IV were sold.

In 1971 the the 455 cu in, 325hp HO V-8 was the standard Trans Am engine, coupled to a 3-speed manual trans with a Hurst floor shifter. 2,116 were sold. Standard equipment included: Vinyl bucket seats, New Endura nose with integral bumpers, front rear wheel opening flares, functional front fender air extractors, rear deck spoiler, dual racing mirrors (left hand remote), concealed wipers, black textured grille, hood scoop with rear facing air intake controlled by the throttle, power cooling fan, power steering, Rallye gauges (clock and tach) formula sport steering wheel, Safe-T-Track differential, power brakes disc front and drum rear, white letter tires, honey-comb wheels, and a four barrel carburetor. The Firebird Trans Am would continue to be offered through the 1974 model year.

All rise for The Judge.

The Judge. From Pontiac.

A new name. With a special brand of justice to discourage the so-called performance-minded competition.

Like a standard, 366-horse, 400-cubic-inch V-8 with Ram Air and a 4-barrel. Or a 370-horse, 400-cube Ram Air IV V-8, if you so order. Either way, those hood scoops function.

Like a fully synchronized, floor-mounted, 3-speed cogbox. A close-ratio 4-speed with Hurst shifter (yea!) and a 3-speed Turbo Hydra-matic (boo!) are also in the hopper, if you'd care to order same.

Like a 60" air foil, blackened grille, exposed headlamps, fiber-glass belted tires (big and black), steel mag-type wheels, blue-red-yellow striping and Judge I.D. inside and out.

Like an Endura schnoz that regards chips, dings and scrapes as acts of treason.

Like Morrokide-covered buckets. And a no-nonsense instrument panel that fills you in. In detail.

Order a hood-mounted tach and power front disc brakes.

Our case rests. It's justice, man.

THE JUDGE

Pontiac Motor Division.

4 color pictures of our '69 Break Away Squad, specs, book jackets and decals are yours for 30¢ (50¢ outside U.S.A.). Write: '69 Wide-Tracks, P.O. Box 888SI, 196 Wide-Track Blvd., Pontiac, Mich. 48056.

1970 Pontiac GTO Judge Fastback

1970 Pontiac GTO Judge Fastback powered by a 455 cu in, 360hp V-8 with 500 ft lb of torque coupled to a 4-speed manual trans was capable of 0-60 in 6.6 sec and the quarter mile in 15 seconds. Cost of the Judge package $332. The GTO so equipped was priced at $3.604 Four port dual exhausts, rear deck spoiler, anti-sway bar, and Rallye wheels: were standard.

The Judge package trim features: Dual hood scoops, Hood mount tach and rear deck spoiler.

The 1970 Pontiac GTO interior shown here with: vinyl covered high back bucket seats, sport steering wheel, padded dash, center console with floor shifter, Hydramatic trans, factory A/C, power windows, power brakes, full set of gauges including tachometer and seat belts.

1970 GTO 455 cu in, 360hp HO V-8. Note: air cleaner, hood scoop air induction collar seal.

1970 Pontiac GTO Judge Convertible

1970 Pontiac GTO Judge Convertible was priced at $4,070 and a total of only 17 were sold.

1970 Pontiac GTO Judge convertible interior with the same features as the fastback coupe.

1970 Pontiac Trans AM Fastback

1970 Pontiac Trans AM featured: Endura rubber front grille surround, split recessed black grille, front air damn, split side marker lights, wheel flares, dual racing side mirrors, special racing stripe, recessed Rallye wheels, black raised letter tires, rear deck integrated spoiler, dual exhausts, Trans Am badging, hood scoop and front fender air induction. Priced at $4,305

1970 Pontiac Trans AM interior; vinyl covered bucket seats with head rests, center console with floor shifter, sport steering wheel, padded dash, engine turned dash insert panel, full set of gauges, including tach, seat belts, full carpeting and optional Hydramatic transmission.

1970 Pontiac Trans AM 400 cu in, 335hp, Ram Air II, HO V-8 engine with 450 ft lb of torque.

1971 Pontiac Trans AM

1971 Pontiac Trans AM was unchanged, standard engine was the LS5 455 cu in HO 335 hp, V-8. With 500 ft lbs of torque could do the quarter mile in 15 sec. It was priced at $4.454.

1971 Trans AM styling continued to use the Endura rubber grille surround and front air dam. The the rear deck spoiler, web cast Rallye wheels and dual exhaust system was standard.

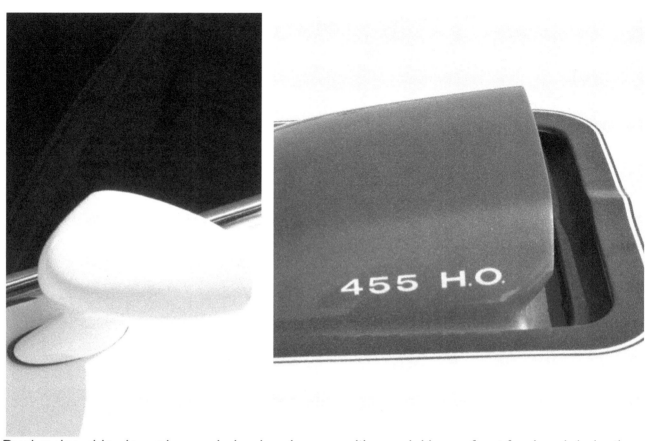

Dual racing side view mirrors, shaker hood scoop with special logo, front fender air induction and cast wheels with narrow white wall raised letter tires and special badging was standard.

1971 Tans AM interior shown with cloth / vinyl high back bucket seats, center console with floor shifter, optional Hydramatic trans, padded dash, remote drive side mirror, seat belts, padded dash with aluminum panel insert, logo floor mats and tilt steering column.,

1970 Pontiac GTO Judge

Wheelbase: 112 inches	Engine: 400 cu in, 366hp V-8*		3-speed manual transmission^	
Model		Price**		Built**
242 Fastback Coupe		$3,840		357
242 Convertible Coupe		4.070		17

*370hp Ram Air V-8
^ Optional 4-speed manual and Hydramatic
**Pricing and production information from Standard catalog of Pontiac by John A. Gunnell

Standard Equipment
Vinyl bucket seats, Padded Dash, Twin air scoops, Heavy duty clutch, Sports springs and shocks, Dual exhausts, DeLuxe steering wheel, T-handle floor shifter, Fiberglass tires, Rallye wheels, Rear deck air foil, Judge stripes and decals, Black textured grille

Optional Equipment
Air conditioning, Cruise control, Power front bucket seats, Power windows, Power brakes, Rear window defogger, Am radio, AM/FM stereo radio.

1970 Pontiac Trans Am

Wheelbase: 108.2 inches	Engine: 400 cu in, 335hp V-8*		3-speed manual transmission.^	
Model		Price		Built
228 Fastback Coupe		$4,305		3,196**

*Available option Ram Air IV 370hp V-8
** Breaks down as; 3,108 Ram Air III 335hp and 88 Ram Air IV 345hp
^Optional 4-speed manual, 2-speed automatic or 3-speed automatic

1971 Pontiac Trans Am

Wheelbase: 108.2 inches	Engine: 455 cu in, 370hp, Ram Air IV HO V-8		3-speed man. Transmission**	
Model		Price		Built
228 Fastback Coupe		$4,464		2,116

**Included a Hurst floor shifter. Optional 4-speed manual or Turbo Hydra-matic

Standard Equipment
(1970) Front air dams, Rear spoiler, Shaker hood, Side air extractors, Dual racing mirrors,Left hand remote side mirror, Front and rear stabilizers, Heavy-duty shocks and springs, Engine turned dash inserts, Rallye gauge cluster, Concealed wipers, Vinyl bucket seats, full carpeting, Power brakes, Power steering, 15 inch Rallye rims, White letter tires, Full length racing stripes.(1971) Sport steering wheel, Rallye gauge cluster, Electric clock and Tachometer, Front air dam, Rear deck spoiler, Wheel well flares, Shaker hood, Honeycomb rims, Black textured grille inserts, Power steering, Power brakes, front discs and rear drums, Front and rear stabilizer, High rate rear springs, Heavy duty shocks, Safe-T-Track differential, Air cleaner with rear facing air induction, Power flex cooling fan, Raised letter tires. Functional fender air extractors. Air cleaner with rear facing air intake on hood controlled by throttle power

Optional Equipment
(1970) Air conditioning, Cruise control, Rear window defroster, Tinted glass, Tinted Windshield, Remote deck lid release, Power front bucket seats. AM radio, AM/FM stereo radio, Stereo tape player, Power door locks, Tilt steering. (1971) Air conditioning, Automatic level control, Cruise control, Tinted glass, Tinted windshield, Cornering lights, AM/FM stereo radio and tape system, Tilt steering.

Production, pricing and equipment information from Standard Catalog of Pontiac and Standard Catalog of Firebird by John A. Gunnell and Encyclopedia of American Cars by Editors of Consumer Guide and www.wikipedia.com

Plymouth Hemi 'Cuda 426
1971

Plymouth introduced the Barracuda on April 1, 1964, two weeks before the Mustang. It was a restyled Valiant, with a new roof and wrap around rear window and deck lid. Which was its unique feature. The 106 wheelbase car was powered by a 170 cu in "Six" or an optional 273 cu in V-8. Coupled to a 3-speed manual or TorqueFlite automatic. On the inside, bucket seats were standard

But unlike the Mustang the Barracuda was unmistakably a Valiant. Whereas the Mustang, based on the Falcon, was an entirely new car, with the only recognizable Falcon feature, the dashboard. The Mustang was a phenomenal success, setting an all time sales record. 500,000 cars in the first six months and 1 million in its first full year. Which prompted other manufacturers to enter the so called "Pony Car" market. The Barracuda sold 23,456 in its first year. Who knows what might have been had the Barracuda been a fresh new body design.

In 1967 the second generation Barracuda was introduced, The wheel base had been stretched to 108" although it still shared some of the Valiant under pinnings, the design was all new and a break away from the Valiant look. In addition a convertible and hardtop were added. The Barracuda was now powered by a 225 cu in Six or a 273 cu in V-8. Over 65,000 were sold.

The third generation Barracuda debuted in 1970, with a new design that wiped away anything in common with the Valiant. The Barracuda was now a full series with three sub series. The standard Barracuda series, the Gran Coupe series and the 'Cuda series. There were two 'Cuda models a Hardtop Coupe and a Convertible Coupe, for the first time a 426 cu in Hemi V-8 was available, with a 4-speed transmission and floor shifter. Bucket seats and special paint and stripping was standard. The Transmission option was a 3-speed TorqueFlite automatic. Little was changed for 1971 except for the grille taillights and interior trim. A one year only feature were quad head lights. Engine options included: a 270 V-8, a 335hp V-8 a 390 V-8 and the monster 426hp Hemi V-8. In addition to special paint colors and striping there was the heavy-duty Dana 60 ring gear, Two models available were the Hardtop Coupe which sold 6,228 units and the Convertible which sold 374 units. The exact number with the 426 cu in, 425hp Hemi V-8 is unknown.

The Barracuda continued through 1974 , but the convertible was dropped after 1971 and the Big block V-8's, together with heavy duty suspensions and rear axles were no longer available. Government mandated emission and mileage standards were taking their toll. The era of Big Engines and unleashed horsepower was over.

1971 Plymouth Hemi 'Cuda 426 Coupe

1971 Plymouth 'Cuda Hemi Coupe was priced at $3,156. The rear window louver was optional along with the driving lights. The unique striping, wide tries , Rally wheels, shaker hood with hood pins and spoiler and dual racing mirrors were standard.

1971 'Cuda rear deck spoiler was standard, rear window louvers driving lights were optional.

The 1971 'Cuda Coupe interior featured: vinyl covered bucket seats. Sport wheel, tilt steering, and floor shifter were standard. A unique full length center console, wall-to-wall carpeting, automatic TorqueFlite, power steering, power windows and power seats were optional.

1971 Plymouth 'Cuda Hemi 426 Convertible

The 1971 Plymouth 'Cuda Hemi Convertible, priced at $3,412 of the 374 sold the exact number equipped with the 426 cu in V-8 are unknown. Last year for the 'Cuda convertible.

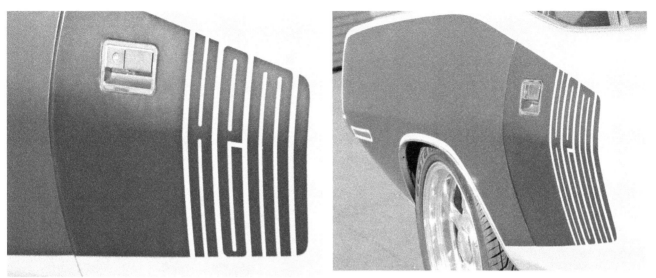

The special decals, striping and functional shaker hood with Hemi 'Cuda emblem; standard.

1971 'Cuda 426 Hemi convertible interior: shown with full length center console, floor "T" shifter Vinyl covered bucket seats, sport steering wheel, TorqueFlite automatic AM/FM stereo radio, tilt steering, wall-to-wall cut pile carpeting and swing out under dash writing table. Wood dash insert, full instrumentation, padded dash, column lock ignition switch.

The 1971 Plymouth Hemi 'Cuda, 426 cu in, 425hp Hemi V-8 Last year for this engine.

1971 Plymouth Hemi 'Cuda 426

Wheelbase: 108 inches	Engine: 426 cu in, 425hp Hemi V-8		4-speed manual Trans.*
Model		Price	Built
BS23	Hardtop Coupe	$4,384.	N/A
BS27	Convertible Coupe	4,640.	N/A

*Optional 3-speed TorqueFlite automatic.

Note: Because of the high cost of the 426 engine package ($1,228) very few were sold. The exact number is not available.

Standard Equipment
Shaker hood, Elastomeric colored bumpers, Heavy-duty ring gear, Upgraded suspension and structural reinforcements, rocker sill moldings, Color keyed grille, Black finished rear deck, 4-speed manual gear box, Heavy-duty Power brakes, Hood pins..

Optional Equipment
Air conditioning, Electric clock, Center console, Side view racing mirrors with remote control, Power door locks, Power steering, Power side windows, Inside hood release, AM/FM radio with stereo and tape. TorqueFlite automatic.

Pricing and equipment information from the Standard Catalog of Chrysler by John A. Gunnell and www.wikipedia.com

References and Resources

Standard Catalog of Chrysler
By John A. Gunnell

Encyclopedia of American Cars
By Editors of Consumer Guide

Standard Catalog of Ford
By John A Gunnell

Standard Catalog of Chevrolet
By John A. Gunnell

Standard Catalog of American Cars
By John A Gunnell

Standard Catalog of Firebird
By John A. Gunnell

Standard Catalog of Buick
By Mary Sieber and Ken Buttolph

Standard Catalog of Pontiac
By John A. Gunnell

American Muscle
By Randy Leffingwell

A Muscle Car Profile
HowStuffWorks

Muscle Cars
www.wikipedia

American Motors
By Patrick Foster

Mopar Muscle
By Robert Genet & David Newhardt

Chevrolet Camaro
GM Heritage Center

The Amazing Boss 429
By Wal Marshall

Boss 429 Performance
Stephen B. Strange

Standard Catalog of American Muscle Cars
John A. Gunnell

Muscle Oldsmobiles
Thomas Bonsall

Detroit Public Library/ Auto Archives
Detroit, Michigan

Ford Motor Auto Museum
Dearborn, Michigan

Mighty Mopars
By Tony Young

Plymouth Barracuda
Doug Zwick & Lanny Knutson

Other Titles......

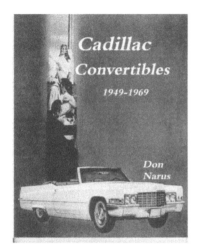
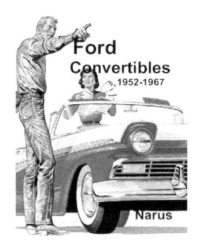
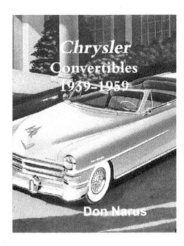

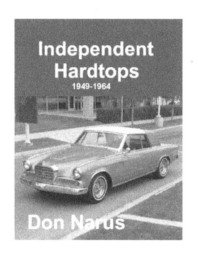
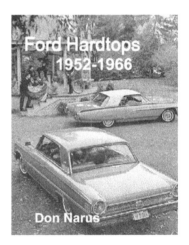

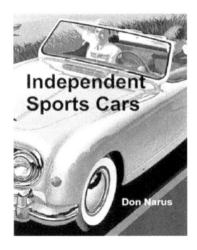
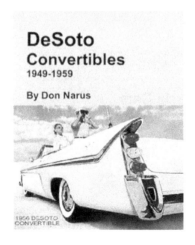
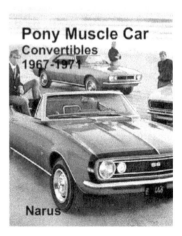

These and other titles are available from www.newalbanybooks.com, or www.LuLu.com
or may be ordered from your favorite book seller

About the Author.....

Don Narus is an auto historian who has chronicled American cars over the last four decades. His interest lies in the history and evolution of the American car. He writes in a relaxed, conversational style. His books focus on the details and nuances of each model, putting you behind the wheel. Its the perfect primer and quick reference guide.

What others have said......

Independent Sports Cars, delivers on what the title promises. Postwar sports cars like AMX, Avanti, Crosley Hot Shot, Delorean, Hudson Italia, Javelin, Kaiser-Darrin, Nash-Healey, as well as Packard and Studebaker Hawks are featured. All are illustrated with black and white vintage and contemporary images. Nine chapters take the reader from and rear of the vehicles, as well as the interiors, dashboards, engine bays and trunks. Author Don Narus accessible style provides interesting anecdotes on each featured car. At the end of each chapter are specifications and production figures. Michael Petti, K-F News Bulletin

Independent Hardtops. The latest title in automotive historian Don Narus's ever expanding library focuses on Studebaker, Packard, Hudson, Nash, Kaiser-Fraser and Willys. Like his other car books this 107 page softcover features brief histories, handy charts with pricing and basic specifications and more than 200 black and white images. It's an inexpensive handy, quick reference. M. McCourt, Hemmings Classic Car

Notes

CPSIA information can be obtained
at www.ICGtesting.com
Printed in the USA
BVHW022126170423
662547BV00006B/31

9 781387 424306